Awesome ENGINEERING

TRAINS, PLANES AND SHIPS

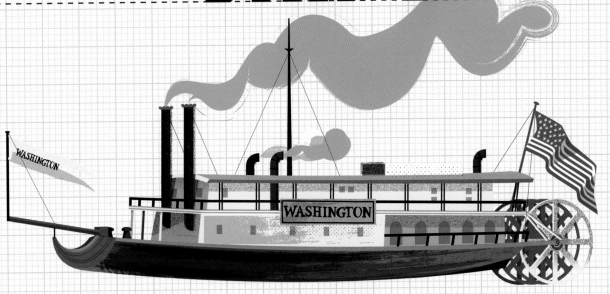

SALLY SPRAY
WITH ARTWORK BY MARK RUFFLE

W
FRANKLIN WATTS
LONDON · SYDNEY

Franklin Watts

First published in Great Britain in 2017
by The Watts Publishing Group
Copyright © The Watts Publishing Group, 2017

Series editor: Paul Rockett
Series design and illustration: Mark Ruffle
www.rufflebrothers.com
Consultant:
Andrew Woodward BEng (Hons) CEng MICE FCIArb

HB ISBN 978 1 4451 5531 9
PB ISBN 978 1 4451 5532 6

Printed in China

Franklin Watts
An imprint of
Hachette Children's Group
Part of The Watts Publishing Group
Carmelite House
50 Victoria Embankment
London EC4Y 0DZ
An Hachette UK Company
www.hachette.co.uk
www.franklinwatts.co.uk

Every attempt has been made to
clear copyright. Should there be any
inadvertent omission please apply to
the publisher for rectification.

Picture credits: Cyo bo/Shutterstock:
23; DPA/Alamy: 29c; Everett Historical/
Shutterstock: 8, 15; Derek Gordon/
Shutterstock: 27; Frederic Legrand-
COMEO/Shutterstock: 29cl; © The Mary
Rose Trust: 7; Meoita/Shutterstock: 11;
Sean Pavone/Shutterstock: 18; Sorbis/
Shutterstock: 25; Simon Taylor/Dreamstime:
21; Topical Press/Hulton Archive/Getty
Images: 28cr; Wikimedia Commons: 28cl,
28c; David Woolfenden/Shutterstock: 13;
Yolanta/Shutterstock: 29cr.

GLARE is a registered trademark of
Structural Laminates Company.

CONTENTS

4 On the Move

6 Mary Rose

8 Washington Paddle Steamer

10 Stephenson's Rocket

12 SS Great Britain

14 Wright Flyer

16 Heinkel He 178

18 Shinkansen Bullet Train

20 Concorde

22 Shanghai Maglev Train

24 Airbus A380

26 USS Gerald R Ford (CVN-78)

28 Fascinating Facts

30 Further Information

31 Glossary

32 Index

ON THE MOVE

Trains, planes and ships transport people and goods all over the world. This timeline highlights key moments in their evolution.

Timeline key

9000 8000 7000 6000

BOATS

8200–7600 BCE
The oldest boat ever found is the Pesse canoe, a dugout tree-trunk canoe found in the Netherlands.

1550–300 BCE
The Phoenicians (who lived in modern-day Lebanon and Syria) and Greeks made wooden galley boats powered by oars.

900 CE
Viking longships were made from wood and powered by oars and sails. The hull was wide and could sail on both rivers and the sea.

1511
Mary Rose (see pages 6–7)

1800s
Tall, streamlined, sailing ships, called clippers, were used to transport cargoes of tea from China. They had many sails and were very fast.

TRAINS

1550s
Rail tracks were first used as a way to move carts carrying heavy loads. Horses or people pulled the carts over rails made from wood, and later iron.

1801
Richard Trevithick invents his first steam locomotive: the Puffing Devil. In 1804, his Penydarren locomotive is the first to run on tracks. And in 1808, the Catch-me-who-can becomes the first train to carry paying passengers.

1829
Stephenson's Rocket (see pages 10–11)

1829
The Stourbridge Lion, the first steam engine to be tested in the USA, ran in Honesdale Pennsylvania. It was made in England and shipped to its new home.

1863
The first underground steam train system opened in London. It was called the Metropolitan Railway.

PLANES

c.1010
Eilmer, a monk from Malmesbury Abbey, attached wings to his arms and leapt from the abbey tower. It's recorded that he flew for 15 seconds, travelling 200 m.

1890
Gustave Trouvé built an ornithopter (a craft that flaps its wings) that flew for 80 m. The wings were powered by small gunpowder explosions.

1903
Wright Flyer (see pages 14–15)

1927
Charles Lindbergh made the first solo flight across the Atlantic in his plane Spirit of St Louis – a single-engined plane with an aerodynamic design.

1930
Frank Whittle invented the jet engine in Great Britain. In 1941, it was tested in the Gloster E.28/39, the first British aircraft with a jet engine.

5000	4000	3000	2000	1000	1000	1100	1200	1300	1400	1500	1600	1700	1800	1900	2000

0

BCE | CE

1816
Washington paddle steamer (see pages 8–9)

1819
SS Savannah is the first steamship to cross the Atlantic Ocean. This wooden ship had sail power and steam-driven side paddles.

1843
SS Great Britain (see pages 12–13)

1911
RMS Titanic, one of the most famous ships of all time, was launched. The enormous passenger liner sank on its first voyage, on 15 April 1912, after colliding with an iceberg.

2013
USS Gerald R Ford aircraft carrier (see pages 26–27)

2015
The world's largest cruise ship, Harmony of the Seas, was launched. It can carry 5,479 passengers, and has a theatre, climbing walls and an ice rink!

1879
The first electric passenger locomotive was shown in Berlin. They became popular in the 1890s, powered by a third electric rail or overhead electric cables.

1883
The Orient Express began running between Paris and Constantinople (now Istanbul). It offered luxury travel for passengers to exotic destinations.

1920s
Diesel locomotives become widespread. They have engines that burn diesel oil to power electric motors. They are more powerful than steam trains and cause less pollution.

1964
Shinkansen (bullet) train (see pages 18–19)

2002
Shanghai Maglev train (see pages 22–23)

1933
The Boeing 247 revolutionises air travel by providing safe, comfortable, long-distance travel for ten passengers!

1937
A modified Lockheed Electra, the XC-35, flies with a pressurised cabin, allowing people to fly without oxygen masks.

1939
Heinkel He 178 (see pages 16–17)

1969
The Hawker Siddeley Harrier, or Jump Jet, is the first plane able to take off vertically. It can hover and fly in any direction – even backwards!

1969
Concorde (see pages 20–21)

2005
Airbus 380 (see pages 24–25)

MARY ROSE

Launched in 1511, the *Mary Rose* was part of the Tudor king Henry VIII's navy. After many years of eventful service and one rebuild in 1536, she sank during the Battle of the Solent in 1545. But that was not the end of her story. In 1971, the wreck was discovered and – 11 years later – raised from the seabed.

BUILDING BRIEF

Build a large, state-of-the-art warship to expand the Royal Navy and defend England's shores.

Location: Portsmouth, England

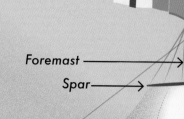

600 MIGHTY OAKS

The *Mary Rose* was a large carrack ship. Carracks are large wooden ships with tall masts and extra decks built up at the bow (front) and stern (rear). The *Mary Rose* was built from high quality oak. It is estimated that over 600 oak trees would have been needed to construct this mighty ship.

STABILITY

The hull is the watertight body of the ship below the deck, and the hull of the *Mary Rose* was filled with a heavy load of gravel (ballast). This kept the ship balanced and the centre of gravity low. On its final voyage the ship was overloaded with guns, making her top heavy. It's thought that the *Mary Rose* made a sharp turn, making the ship lean, putting the gun ports below the waterline, flooding the hull and causing her to sink.

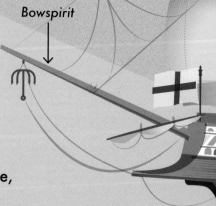

Foremast →

Spar →

Bowspirit

SPEED AND STEERING

Weighing around 453 tonnes, the Mary Rose was not quick or agile. Steering and speed were controlled by the masts and sails. Sails of different shapes and sizes caught the wind, with the wind's pressure on the sails pushing the ship along. Ropes (rigging) attached to the masts could angle the position of the sails in the direction that would best catch the wind and aid the ship's steering.

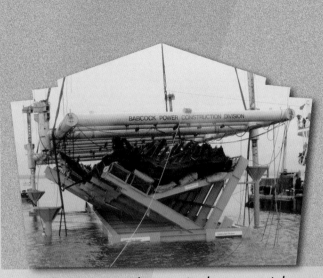

The Mary Rose being raised on a special cradle in 1982.

Main mast ←

Mizzen ←

Bonaventure mizzen ←

Triangular lateen sail ←

Gun ports ←

Length 45 m

CLINKER OR CARVEL?

After the ship was raised, it was possible to see which timbers were original and which had been replaced during repairs in 1536. Two techniques of construction were used to build the wooden hull:

The clinker or clench method of shipbuilding, was older. The overlapping planks were secured by nails, driven through the overlaps and bent over the edges. Cutting holes for guns weakened the structure.

The carvel method was more modern in 1536. Edge-to-edge planks were fastened to a supporting wooden frame. Caulking made from horsehair and thin rope filled the gaps, and a waterproof layer of pitch was added.

Clinker

Carvel

WASHINGTON PADDLE STEAMER

In the 19th century, paddle steamers became a common sight on the Mississippi river in the USA. They moved large numbers of people and vast quantities of freight, playing a significant part in the commercial development of the ten states through which the river runs. The *Washington* was one of the fastest paddle steamers of all. It was launched in 1816, during the golden age of paddle power.

BUILDING BRIEF

Design and build a ship for carrying cargo and passengers. It must be powerful enough to sail against strong river currents and to stay afloat in the shallows.

Engineer: Henry Shreve

Location: Wheeling, West Virginia, USA

The author Mark Twain (1835–1910) worked as a river pilot on a paddle steamer. He wrote: 'Piloting on the Mississippi river was not work to me; it was play, delightful play, adventurous play ... and I loved it ...'

CONSTRUCTION

Constructed from wood, the bottom of the ship was flat so it could sail in shallow water. Iron rods, called hog chains, were connected to the hull at either end. Hog chains could be tightened with a turnbuckle. The tension in the chains made the keel bend downwards and pressure from the water below pushed upwards. These opposite forces kept the bottom flat.

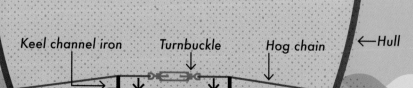

Keel channel iron   Turnbuckle   Hog chain   ←Hull

Water pressure

STEAM POWER

The *Washington's* steam engine was positioned towards the rear of the ship, near to the paddle. The fire room and boiler were positioned near the front to balance the weight of the vessel.

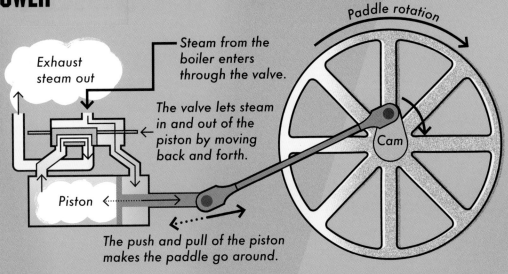

Exhaust steam out

Steam from the boiler enters through the valve.

The valve lets steam in and out of the piston by moving back and forth.

Paddle rotation

Cam

Piston

The push and pull of the piston makes the paddle go around.

Steam engines have a few simple components. The firebox is where a fire is lit and fed. The boiler is where water boils when heated by the fire, to give off steam. The steam is sent to rod-and-piston mechanisms that are connected to the paddle. As the steam pressure rises, it fills the piston cavity and moves the piston rods, which turn the paddle.

PADDLE

The *Washington* is described as a sternwheeler, meaning that the single large driving paddle is at the stern (the rear) of the ship. The paddle was a large wooden frame, with two circles of wood at each end separated by spaced blades. When the wheel structure is turned by the engine, the blades cut into the water and scoop it backwards to generate the thrust to move the boat along. About a quarter of the wheel enters the water at any one time.

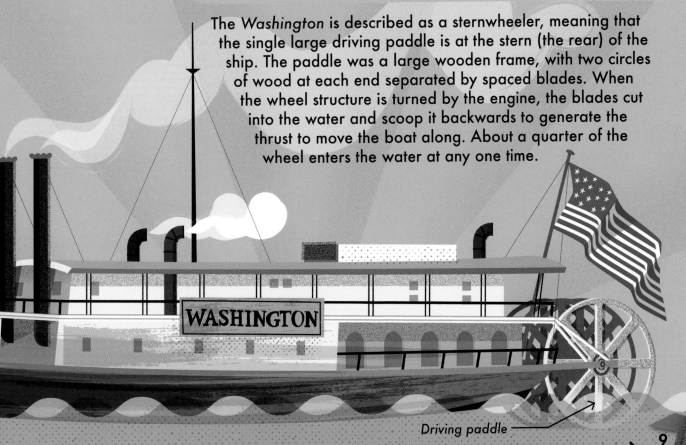

WASHINGTON

Driving paddle

Length 57 m

STEPHENSON'S ROCKET

In 1829, a competition called the Rainhill Trials was held in Merseyside in the UK. Its aim was to find the best steam locomotive of the day. The *Rocket* was the only locomotive to finish the trial. The prize was the contract to build steam engines to run on the Liverpool and Manchester Railway.

BUILDING BRIEF

Design and build a reliable steam locomotive able to pull carriages for freight and passengers, to work the newly completed railway line between Liverpool and Manchester.

Engineers: George Stephenson and his son Robert Stephenson

Location: Rainhill, Merseyside, UK

MULTI-TUBE BOILER

Earlier steam engines had just one or two pipes that carried the heat from the fire to the water tank. Instead, Stephenson's design featured a multi-tube boiler with 25 copper pipes. This allowed the water in the tank to heat up more quickly making his locomotive faster and more fuel-efficient.

BLAST PIPE

Steam out of the piston is fed into the chimney through the blast pipe. In doing so, this draws hot air out of the firebox through the pipes in the boiler. This is where the 'chuffing' of steam trains comes from as smoke and steam is blown out of the chimney with every stroke of the pistons.

A replica of Stephenson's Rocket

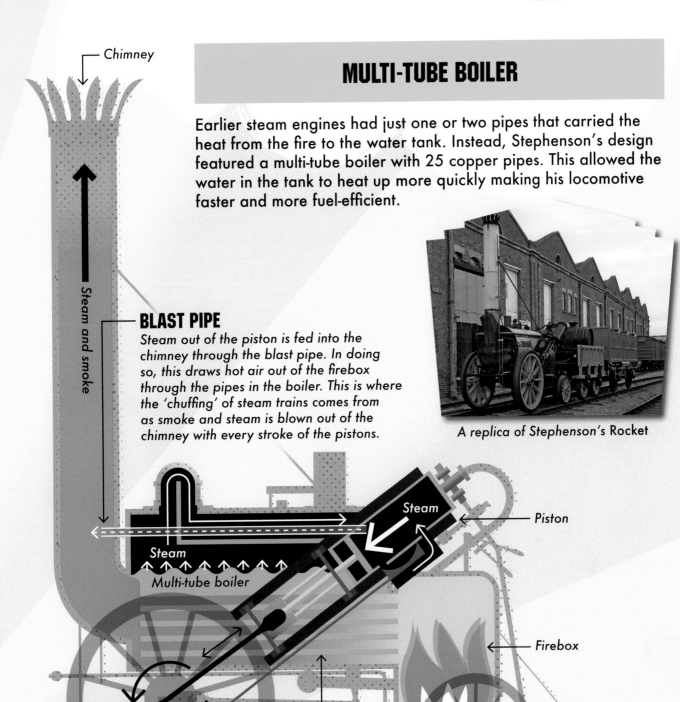

Chimney

Steam and smoke

Steam

Steam

Multi-tube boiler

Piston

Firebox

Boiling water

Pistons drive the wheels

BLUEPRINT

The *Rocket* was designed specifically to be fast and lightweight, to pull passengers rather than coal or other freight. It was not the first steam locomotive, but it was the most successful of the time and led to the growth of passenger railway networks. It became the blueprint for locomotive design for the next 150 years.

SS GREAT BRITAIN

Isambard Kingdom Brunel, the ingenious Victorian engineer, brought together the most modern ideas of shipbuilding and put them all into the massive SS *Great Britain*. Launched in 1843, it was the longest passenger ship in the world and the first steamship made from iron.

BUILDING BRIEF

Build a ship using all the latest technology to carry passengers and freight across the Atlantic Ocean, between the UK and the USA.

Engineer: Isambard Kingdom Brunel

Designer: Thomas Guppy

Location: Bristol, UK

Atlantic Ocean

In 1845, she became the first steam-powered iron ship to cross the Atlantic. The voyage took just over two weeks.

The ship was powered by two enormous steam engines, but it also got an extra push from wind power. There were large sails on six iron masts that could be lowered on iron hinges when not in use.

Length 98 m

IRON

At first, the SS *Great Britain*'s hull was to be made from wood. But when Brunel saw the *Rainbow* – an iron-hulled ship – he changed his mind. Brunel recognised that there are many advantages gained by using iron instead of wood:
- iron is stronger than wood and not in danger from dry rot or woodworm;
- in the 19th century, iron was in ready supply, while wood was expensive and harder to find for such large projects.

By the end of the planning process, the engineers had designed a monumental ship. It would be 98 m in length and weigh 1,961 tonnes. This was heavier than any other ship in the world!

You can visit the SS Great Britain in Bristol, UK.

PROPELLER POWER

On his previous ships, Brunel had used paddlewheels to push vessels through the water. This time he decided to go with a screw propeller. The propeller is submerged under the waterline, near the base of the hull. This position means that the ship is more stable in rough seas, and more streamlined, rather than having paddles placed either side of the hull.

Drive shaft

A propeller is a circular structure of blades spinning on a drive shaft positioned at the rear of the boat. As it spins it creates a difference in pressure at the front and back of the propeller. The churned water behind creates a force that pushes the boat forward.

WRIGHT FLYER

On 17 December 1903, the Wright brothers made history when their aircraft – the *Wright Flyer* – lifted from the ground. The first powered flight lasted just 12 seconds and the *Wright Flyer* flew only 36.5 m, but the new age of flight had begun!

BUILDING BRIEF

Be the first in the world to build and pilot a flying machine that can make a controlled and powered flight, and change the future of modern transport!

Engineers: Wilbur and Orville Wright

Location: Kitty Hawk, North Carolina, USA

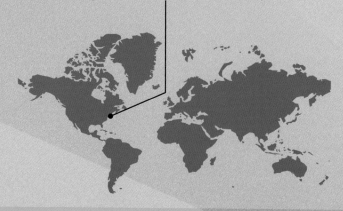

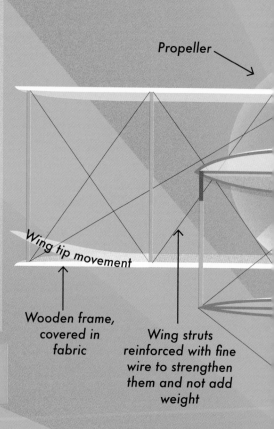

Propeller

Wing tip movement

Wooden frame, covered in fabric

Wing struts reinforced with fine wire to strengthen them and not add weight

FROM BICYCLE TO BIPLANE

Wilbur and Orville Wright had been interested in mechanics and engineering for most of their lives. They ran a bicycle manufacture and repair shop, and believed that cycling and flying relied on similar factors:
- the ability to balance and control the machine;
- a strong but lightweight frame;
- a chain and sprocket propulsion system;
- and a need for wind resistance and aerodynamics to increase speed.

The Wright Flyer *had a petrol engine that powered a chain and sprocket device, like that on a bicycle, which linked to the two propellers.*

TOTAL CONTROL

The success of the *Wright Flyer* was due to the very light engine and the brothers' skill at flying the plane. The different movements, known as pitch, yaw and roll, could all be controlled, allowing for a stable flight.

ROLL

Roll was controlled using a system of pulley ropes. These allowed a twisting movement in the tips of the wings that could increase the lift on one wing and decrease it on the other allowing the plane to bank.

Yaw could be controlled using the rudder.

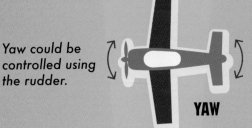

YAW

PITCH

Pitch was adjusted using the elevator control, which could be moved up or down to give more or less lift to the nose.

Rudder

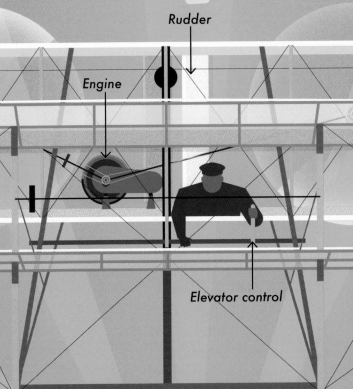

Engine

Wing tip movement

Elevator control

Chain

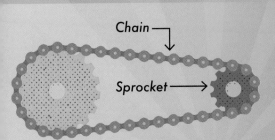

Sprocket

On the day of the flight, Wilbur's attempt failed and it was Orville who made the first recorded powered flight.

HEINKEL HE 178

The first jet-powered plane, the Heinkel He 178, was launched on 27 August 1939. Built as a test plane, it only flew for five minutes. The inventor was forced to stop developing the turbojet technology further, as a week later the Second World War began and the German airforce wanted planes that could fly for much longer. They weren't interested in the Heinkel He 178.

BUILDING BRIEF

Be the first in the world to design and build a practical plane that can usefully harness and control the power of a jet engine.

Engineers: Ernst Heinkel and Dr Hans Pabst von Ohain

Location: Warnemünde, Rostock, Germany

TAKE-OFF

The plane's engine moves the plane forward quickly; this force is called thrust. Air then flows over and under the wings, causing lift. When the lift force is greater than the weight of the plane, it takes off.

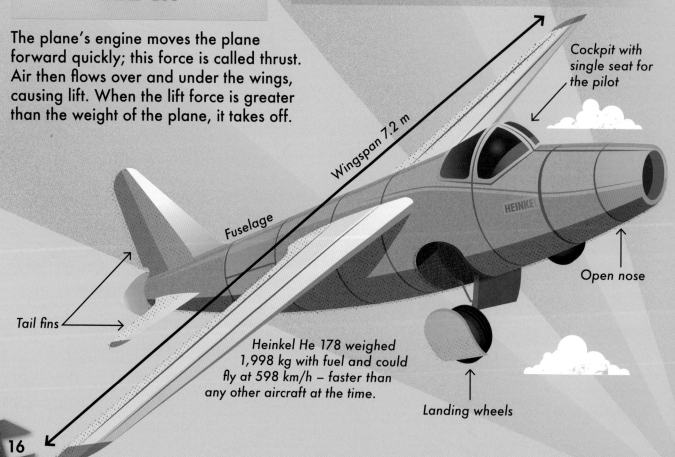

Wingspan 7.2 m

Cockpit with single seat for the pilot

Open nose

Fuselage

HEINKE

Tail fins

Heinkel He 178 weighed 1,998 kg with fuel and could fly at 598 km/h – faster than any other aircraft at the time.

Landing wheels

DESIGN FEATURES

The He 178 had an aerodynamic metal body, curved for maximum airflow. The wings, which were wooden and curved at the ends, were fixed to the top of the fuselage (main body) behind the cockpit. It was a 'tail dragger', with the tail resting on the back landing wheels, near the ground. The single jet engine was hidden in the middle of the plane, behind the pilot. Air was taken in through the open nose to feed oxygen to the jet engine, and the high-powered exhaust fumes shot out of the tail end. While the design was light-weight and sleek, flights could only last up to 10 minutes because the fuel burnt so fast.

HOW A JET ENGINE WORKS

The jet engine had been invented by Sir Frank Whittle in 1930.
The design principles have changed very little since then.

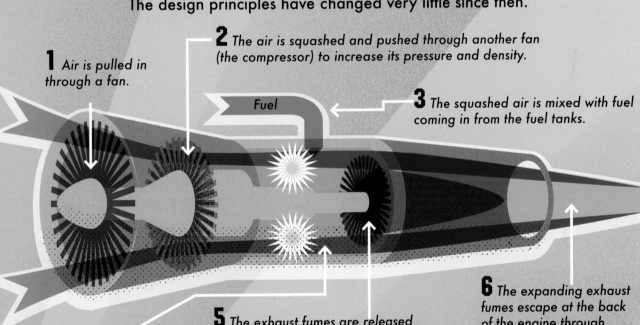

1 *Air is pulled in through a fan.*

2 *The air is squashed and pushed through another fan (the compressor) to increase its pressure and density.*

Fuel

3 *The squashed air is mixed with fuel coming in from the fuel tanks.*

4 *The air and fuel mix is burnt in the combustion chamber; it burns fiercely at high temperatures producing exhaust gases.*

5 *The exhaust fumes are released past a set of turbine blades, sending them spinning. The turbine spins an axle which is connected back through the engine to the fan and compressor at the beginning of the engine.*

6 *The expanding exhaust fumes escape at the back of the engine through an exhaust nozzle, and the push of this escaping stream of high-pressure and high-temperature exhaust fumes powers the plane forwards.*

LATER DEVELOPMENTS

Design basics from the Heinkel He 178 were moved around to improve future aircraft. Two engines were used, one placed under each wing. This increased power and stability, making room in the fuselage for fuel tanks, which increased the flight range. Wings were made longer, improving handling, stability and steering.

SHINKANSEN BULLET TRAIN

In the 1960s, Japan began work on the first rail network built for high-speed electric trains (shinkansen in Japanese). Now, shinkansen trains – also known as bullet trains because of their speed and appearance – zoom along tracks that link the islands of Honshu, Kyushu and Hokkaido.

BUILDING BRIEF

Design a new high-speed network of railways for Japan, to replace the old narrow-gauge system and to help commercial development.

Chief engineer: Hideo Shima

Location: Tokyo

BIRD BEAK

The nose shape of the Shinkansen 500 copied the tapering beak of the kingfisher bird. This aerodynamic design helped improve the train's energy consumption by around 30 per cent, while also reducing noise pollution.

Kingfisher

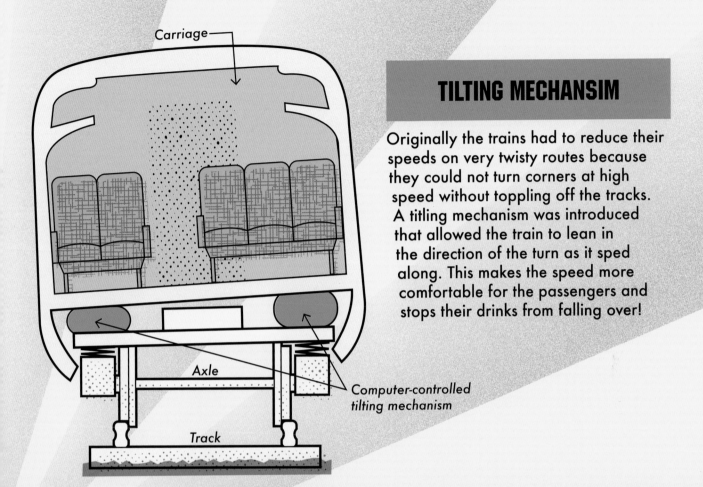

Carriage

TILTING MECHANSIM

Originally the trains had to reduce their speeds on very twisty routes because they could not turn corners at high speed without toppling off the tracks. A titling mechanism was introduced that allowed the train to lean in the direction of the turn as it sped along. This makes the speed more comfortable for the passengers and stops their drinks from falling over!

Axle

Computer-controlled tilting mechanism

Track

BUZZING AXLES

Shinkansen trains are powered by an overhead electric cable. The acceleration and braking of each individual wheel axle is controlled by the electric current. This is a much lighter system than on conventional trains, where one heavy engine car pulls all the carriages and brake pads are used. The reduced weight means shinkansen trains can reach speeds of 270 km/h, and there is less wear and maintenance needed on the track.

CONCORDE

In 1969, the iconic Concorde took to the skies. It was the first passenger plane to fly at supersonic speed, which means faster than the speed of sound. In fact, Concorde flew *twice* as fast as the speed of sound, which meant that you saw it coming way before you heard it.

BUILDING BRIEF

As part of a joint French-British alliance, design and build a supersonic aircraft for super-fast passenger flights around the world.

Engineer: Sir James Hamilton

Location: London, Paris and Bristol where it was built

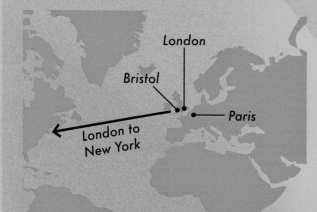

The name 'Concorde', meaning agreement and harmony, was decided upon because the development of the project was a joint French and British initiative.

SUPERSONIC ENGINES

Concorde used four Rolls Royce turbo jet engines, the most powerful jet engines available. They featured 'reheat' technology, an extra stage in the usual jet engine process. This added more fuel to the exhaust fumes produced after the first stage of burning. This exhaust and fuel mix was combusted and the resulting superheated exhaust provided the extra thrust needed for the take-off speed of 400 km/h and to reach the supersonic cruising speed of 2,160 km/h or Mach 2 (another way of saying twice the speed of sound).

ARRIVE BEFORE LEAVING!

The supersonic speed of Concorde meant that it could transport you from London to New York in less than 3.5 hours. So in New York time you would be landing one hour before you took off!

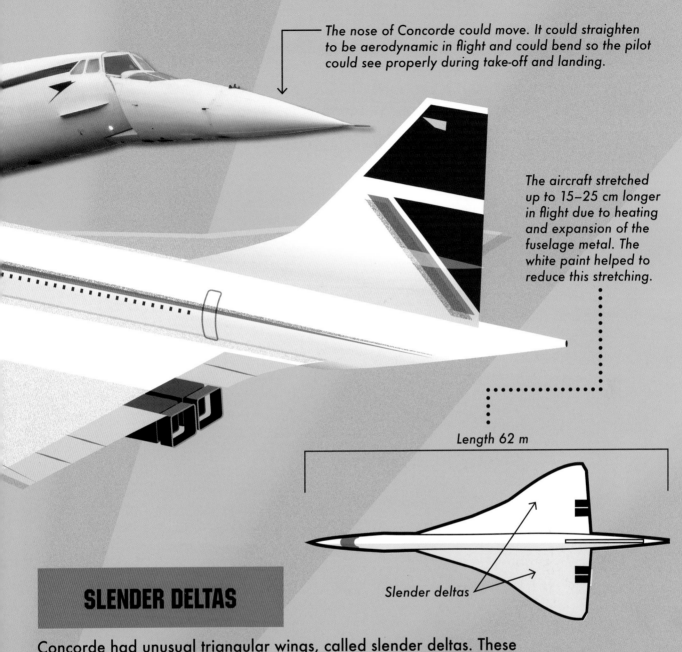

The nose of Concorde could move. It could straighten to be aerodynamic in flight and could bend so the pilot could see properly during take-off and landing.

The aircraft stretched up to 15–25 cm longer in flight due to heating and expansion of the fuselage metal. The white paint helped to reduce this stretching.

Length 62 m

Slender deltas

SLENDER DELTAS

Concorde had unusual triangular wings, called slender deltas. These were a great engineering solution allowing enough wingspan area for Concorde to fly at slower speeds on take-off and landing, but were thin and aerodynamic enough to allow the plane to fly at supersonic speeds. Wings on fast planes don't need to be big, just slim enough to move through the air and maintain lift. Lift is generated by air moving faster over the top of the wings than below.

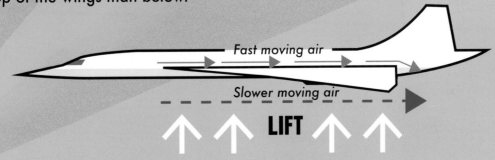

Fast moving air

Slower moving air

LIFT

SHANGHAI MAGLEV TRAIN

The Shanghai maglev train travels just 30 km in each direction, but its magnetic technology means that it can whizz along at speeds of up to 431 km/h, making it the world's fastest train.

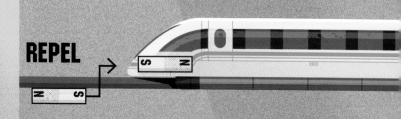

REPEL

BUILDING BRIEF

Design and build a fast rail link from the city airport to provide links to the metro system in Shanghai.

Contractor: Siemens

Location: Shanghai, China

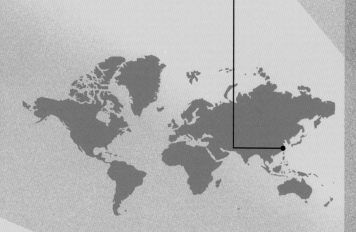

HOW A MAGLEV WORKS

The maglev does not have any wheels. Instead it uses a technology that creates an electromagnetic force in the track. To create this force, the system needs an electrical power source, conductive metal coils in the track, and magnets attached underneath and in the train. The train itself does not need an engine. When the electromagnetic force in the track is activated, it reacts against the magnets on the underside of the train, the two magnets repel each other and the train is levitated 1–10 cm above the track.

MAGNET POWER

To understand maglev's electromagnetic technology, it helps to understand a bit about magnets. Magnets have a north pole and a south pole. If you put the north pole of one and the south pole of another together, they attract and 'stick' together. If you put two north poles, or two south poles together, they repel and try to push apart.

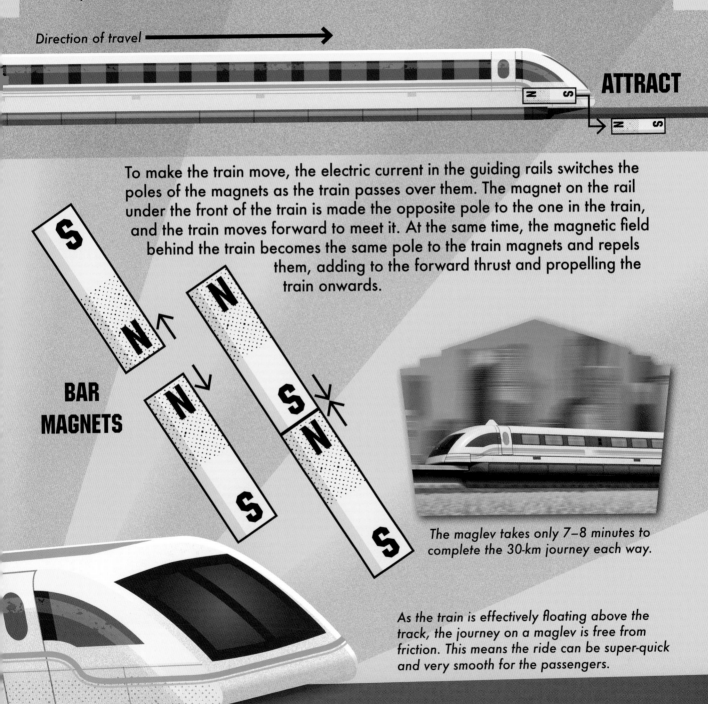

Direction of travel →

ATTRACT

To make the train move, the electric current in the guiding rails switches the poles of the magnets as the train passes over them. The magnet on the rail under the front of the train is made the opposite pole to the one in the train, and the train moves forward to meet it. At the same time, the magnetic field behind the train becomes the same pole to the train magnets and repels them, adding to the forward thrust and propelling the train onwards.

BAR MAGNETS

The maglev takes only 7–8 minutes to complete the 30-km journey each way.

As the train is effectively floating above the track, the journey on a maglev is free from friction. This means the ride can be super-quick and very smooth for the passengers.

AIRBUS A380

The Airbus A380 is the largest passenger jet in service today. It can carry up to 853 passengers on two decks, but despite its size, it has low emissions (waste gases) per passenger and makes less noise at take-off than many smaller planes.

EXHAUSTING ENGINES

Launched in 2005, the Airbus A380 is a giant of the skies, with the best of aircraft design to make it a perfect ride for long-haul flights. It features four turbo fan engines – two on each wing – to give it the lift it needs to leave the ground. Two of the engines are fitted with thrust reversers, which on landing are used to direct engine thrust forwards (rather than backwards) to slow and stop the plane.

The engines can run on kerosene alone or a mix of kerosene and natural gas, which can mean cleaner emissions.

BUILDING BRIEF

Build an aircraft that is very efficient at transporting large numbers of passengers long distances to reduce the cost per seat per kilometre travelled.

Engineer: Jean Roeder

Location: Toulouse, France

Barge
Beluga
Road

Broughton
Filton
Hamburg
Meaulte
Laupheim
Nantes
Toulouse
Getafe
Puerto Real

To construct the plane a special transport network called the Itinéraire à Grand Gabarit had to be organised. To get the large aircraft parts to Toulouse from their factories in Spain, Germany and the UK, waterways and roads had to be widened and special barges, ships and lorries made. Some parts were flown in by a giant Beluga transport plane.

WING TIPS

The wingspan could not be longer than 80 m because of airport restrictions. To compensate for this the Airbus A380 has wing-tip fences at the ends, which are shaped sections pointing up and down at right-angles to the wings. These allow the wings to generate more lift and reduce the drag (opposing force) placed on the craft, providing the benefits of a longer wing without the extra length.

The large inside space allows for more seats, or fewer seats but more luxuries. Some A380 planes have bar areas, social seating, beds and showers!

Wing-tip fence

Wingspan 80 m

MOULDING MATERIAL

As the plane is so big it was important to use light-weight materials that were also incredibly strong. The fuselage is made from sections of aluminium alloys (aluminium mixed with other metals) and plastics.

The upper part of the fuselage is constructed using a material called GLARE®, which is made from layers of aluminium and glass fibre. GLARE® is much lighter and stronger than using metal alone, and can be easily moulded into an aerodynamic shape.

25

USS GERALD R FORD (CVN-78)

Aircraft carriers are phenomenal vehicles, combining sea and air power. They have to be enormous – some are big enough to carry and launch up to 80 aircraft! Launched in 2013, the USS *Gerald R Ford* is a supercarrier, featuring the most up-to-date electrical, computer, radar and electromagnetic technology.

BUILDING BRIEF

Design and build a new aircraft carrier able to sail for months at a time without stopping, providing sea and air defence for the US Navy, fewer crew and better onboard living conditions.

Builders: Newport News Shipbuilding

Location: Norfolk Naval Station, Virginia (home port), USA

The radar system scans for information on different bands, putting all the readings together and displaying them on screen. It can trace smaller and faster objects, and as it has no moving parts it is efficient and easy to maintain.

Advances in computer technology have allowed the command centre, called an island, to be smaller than on previous carriers. It is higher and nearer the stern than earlier aircraft carriers. This allows for more flight-deck space, so aircraft can be launched and landed much more quickly.

Command centre

78

ELECTROMAGNETIC AIRCRAFT LAUNCH SYSTEM (EMALS)

As there is not enough room on an aircraft carrier for planes to take off in the same way they do on land, a special launch system is used. The runway has a built-in track with a shuttle powered by an electromagnetic force, similar to that used in a maglev train. The aircraft is attached to the shuttle by a towbar on the front wheels. When the plane is ready to go, the engines fire and the shuttle runs at high speed along the track, taking the plane with it and launching it off the end of the runway.

QUICK LANDING

When a plane lands on the carrier, its tailhook snags on cables on the deck, bringing the aircraft to a quick halt. The kinetic (moving) energy from the plane is transferred through the steel cables and absorbed by them. An aircraft might come in to land at speeds of over 200 km/h, but it can be stopped in just two seconds!

The tailhook underneath the plane catches on deck cables, bringing the plane to an abrupt halt.

POWER SURGE

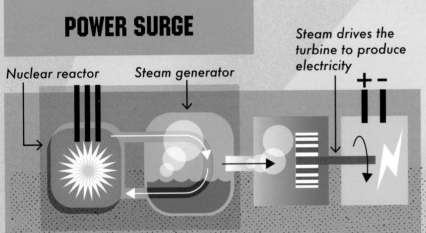

Nuclear reactor Steam generator Steam drives the turbine to produce electricity

The carrier uses a lot of electricity. To generate the power needed, the CVN-78 has two A1B nuclear reactors. These run off energy from a chemical element called uranium.

The uranium atoms split and cause reactions, called fission, within the reactor. This releases heat energy used to boil water, which in turn is used to drive steam turbines to generate electricity. The reactors are smaller than previous models, have fewer parts, requiring less maintenance, but they give out three times more electrical energy.

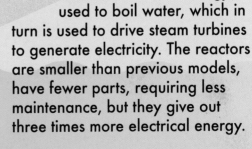

Length 333 m

FASCINATING FACTS

Trains, planes and ships continue to evolve, becoming more and more awesome. Here are more facts about amazing engineers and terrific transport from around the world.

INSPIRATIONAL ENGINEERS

Many women become engineers. Here are the achievements of three pioneering women who worked on trains, planes and ships.

Victoria Drummond *was the first British woman to become a marine engineer. During the Second World War she worked aboard ships and was commended for bravery. After the war she worked as an engineer overseeing shipbuilding.*

Canadian **Elsie MacGill** *was an aeronautical designer. She oversaw the mass production of Hawker Hurricane aircraft during the Second World War. She became know as 'Queen of the Hurricanes'.*

Olive Dennis *was a railroad engineer working in the USA in the 1920s. Her job was to make rail travel more comfortable and appealing. Some of her train improvements included ceiling lights, air-conditioned compartments and reclining seats. These comforts were adopted by rail companies and airlines all over the world.*

The longest train ever to run was an Australian freight train. In 2001, it ran 275 km between Newman and Port Headland, its eight locomotives pulling 682 wagons loaded with iron ore. The train was an astonishing 7.4 km long!

SOLAR POWER

Engineers are looking at new ways to power transport without using fossil fuels. Solar power is one possible solution. Solar panels gather the Sun's energy and convert it into electricity. They absorb photons from sunlight and emit electrons, that give off an electric current, which is stored in batteries.

On 26 July 2016 **Solar Impulse 2** landed in Abu Dhabi, completing the first circumnavigation of the world in an aircraft entirely powered by solar energy. It took 16 months to travel the incredible 42,000 km journey.

The **MS Tûranor PlanetSolar** is the largest solar-powered boat in the world. It's a scientific research vessel used to investigate climate change around the planet. The 809 solar panels on the roof provide all the electricity that the boat needs.

Blackfriars Bridge in London is the biggest solar-powered bridge in the world. Solar provides 50 per cent of the railway station's energy. Solar-powered trains should be coming soon ...

One of the largest vessels in the world is the **Prelude FLNG**. Launched in 2013, it's a whopping 488 m long. It can sail to natural gas fields, drill and extract the gas, turn it into liquid and carry it back to land to be used as fuel. FLNG stands for Floating Liquefied Natural Gas.

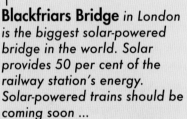

First flying in 1964, the **Lockheed SR-71 Blackbird** is the fastest jet ever. Nicknamed 'Blackbird', it flew 26,000 m above the ground at speeds of up to 3,530 km/h. It was a spy plane that flew too high and fast to be caught.

FURTHER INFORMATION

BOOKS

Amazing Jobs: Engineering by Colin Hyson (Wayland, 2016)

A History of Britain in 12 Feats of Engineering by Paul Rockett (Franklin Watts, 2015)

How to Build: Aircraft by Rita Storey (Franklin Watts, 2016)

It'll Never Work: Cars, Trucks and Trains by Jon Richards (Franklin Watts, 2016)

It'll Never Work: Planes and Helicopters by Jon Richards (Franklin Watts, 2016)

WEBSITES

Search on here for more information on how trains, planes and ships work:
http://science.howstuffworks.com

How steam engines work:
http://www.explainthatstuff.com/steamengines.html

How jet engines work:
http://www.explainthatstuff.com/jetengine.html

How ships float:
http://www.explainthatstuff.com/how-ships-work.html

Every effort has been made by the Publishers to ensure that these websites are suitable for children, that they are of the highest educational value, and that they contain no inappropriate or offensive material. However, because of the nature of the Internet, it is impossible to guarantee that the contents of these sites will not be altered. We strongly advise that Internet access is supervised by a responsible adult.

GLOSSARY

acceleration How quickly an object or vehicle speeds up or slows down.

aerodynamic A shape that reduces drag, allowing the object or vehicle to move through the air more quickly.

airflow The movement (flow) of air around a vehicle.

aluminium A light, strong metal.

architect A person who designs and often supervises the construction of buildings.

blueprint A design plan or technical drawing.

cargo Goods carried by ship, train or lorry.

carrack A large wooden ship dating from the 14th –17th centuries.

centre of gravity The point in an object where all its weight appears to be concentrated.

chain and sprocket A mechanism used on bicycles and consisting of sprockets (toothed wheels) and a linked chain.

commuter A person who regularly travels a distance to work.

components The parts of a machine.

congestion Of traffic, traffic that is slow-moving or stuck in a traffic jam.

current The flow of a river.

designer A person who thinks up ideas and draws out plans.

drag The force of resistance that all objects experience as they travel through air or water.

dry rot A type of wood decay caused by fungi.

electromagnet A metallic core with a metal wire coiled around it, through which an electric current is passed, creating a magnetic field around the wire.

elevator A hinged flap on the tail of an aircraft, used to control motion.

emissions Waste gases, or fumes, that are produced by a working engine.

engineer A person who designs, constructs and maintains buildings, machines and other structures.

exhaust Waste gases from a working machine.

force A push or a pull on an object.

fossil fuels Natural fuels, such as coal, gas or oil, formed from the remains of ancient living things. They are non-renewable.

freight Goods (food, cars, raw materials etc.) transported in bulk by ship, truck, train or aircraft.

friction A force that slows down the movement of a surface that is moving over another.

gravity A force of attraction between all objects. Earth's gravity makes objects fall to the ground and keeps us from floating off into space.

gun port An opening on the side of a ship through which a gun can be fired.

hover To stay suspended in one place in the air.

kerosene A type of fuel oil derived from petroleum.

kinetic energy The energy an object has because it is moving.

lift The upward force produced on the wing (of a plane or an aircraft) as it moves through air.

manoeuvrable Easy to move or steer/guide.

modification A change made to something, usually to improve it.

monumental Big in size and importance.

oars Paddles with a flattened end used to move a boat through water by paddling or rowing.

pilot On a river or at a port, someone who is skilled at guiding a ship along a river or into port.

pioneering New and exciting (ideas/procedure/ work of art).

pollution Dirty or poisonous substances in the air or water.

pulley A grooved wheel with a rope running around it, allowing heavy weights to be lifted more easily.

radar A system that detects the presence, direction, distance and speed of aircraft, ships and other objects by sending out radio waves which are 'bounced' back to the system.

shallows Part of the river where the water is not deep.

solo Something done by one person.

steel A strong, hard metal formed from iron, carbon and other materials.

thrust The pushing force that pushes a vehicle through the air.

timber Wood that has been cut into planks.

uranium A radioactive chemical element.

vortex Swirling motion of water or air.

waterline The level the water reaches along the hull (side or bottom) of a boat.

INDEX

Airbus A380 5, 24–25
aircraft 4–5, 14–17, 20–21, 24–27, 29

Blackfriars Bridge 29

carracks 6–7
carriers, aircraft 5, 26–27
Concorde 5, 20–21

device, chain and sprocket 14

Eilmer 4
electromagnetic aircraft launch system 27
electromagnets 22–23, 26–27
engineers
    Brunel, Isambard Kingdom 12–13
    Dennis, Olive 28
    Drummond, Victoria 28
    Hamilton, Sir James 20–21
    Heinkel, Ernst 16–17
    MacGill, Elsie 28
    Newport News Shipbuilding 26–27
    Roeder, Jean 24–25
    Shima, Hideo 18–19
    Shreve, Henry 8–9
    Siemens 22–23
    Stephenson, George and Robert 4, 10–11
    Trevithick, Richard 4
    von Ohain, Dr Hans Pabst 16–17
    Whittle, Sir Frank 4, 17
    Wright, Orville and Wilbur 4, 14–15
engines
    jet 4, 5, 16–17, 20–21, 24–25, 29
    steam 4–5, 8–13

flight, first powered 4, 14–15

Harmony of the Seas 5
Heinkel He 178 5, 16–17
Henry VIII 6–7

lift 15, 16, 20–21, 24–25
Lindbergh, Charles 4
Lockheed SR-71 Blackbird 29

Mach 2 20–21
Mary Rose 4, 6–7
mechanism, tilting 19
MS Tûranor PlanetSolar 29

Newport News Shipbuilding 26–27

paddle steamers 5, 8–9, 13
pitch 15
Prelude FLNG 29
propellers 13, 14

radar 26
RMS Titanic 5
Rainhill Trials 10–11
Rocket 4, 10–11
roll 15

Second World War 16–17, 28
Shanghai maglev train 5, 22–23
Shinkansen bullet train 5, 18–19
ships
    aircraft carriers 5, 26–27
    nuclear-powered 26–27
    solar-powered 29
    steamships 5, 8–9, 12–13
    wind-powered 4, 6–7, 12–13
    wooden 4–9
Solar Impulse 2 29
SS Great Britain 5, 12–13
SS Savannah 5

thrust 9, 16, 20, 23, 24
trains
    bullet/Shinkansen 5, 18–19
    diesel 5
    electric 5, 18–19
    maglev 22–23, 27
    steam locomotives 4–5, 10–11
Trouvé, Gustave 4
Twain, Mark 8

USS Gerald R Ford 5, 26–27

Washington 5, 8–9
Wright Flyer 4, 14–15

yaw 15

Awesome ENGINEERING

TITLES IN THIS SERIES:

BRIDGES
Get Over It!
Si-o-she Pol
Brooklyn Bridge
Forth Bridge
Vizcaya Bridge
Tower Bridge
Golden Gate Bridge
Governor Albert D Rosellini Bridge
Akashi-Kaikyō Bridge
Juscelino Kubitschek Bridge
Millau Viaduct
The Helix
Fascinating Facts
Further Information
Glossary
Index

FAIRGROUND RIDES
All the Fun of the Fair!
Swingboats
Mauch Chunk Switchback Railway
Carousel
Chair Swing Ride
Ferris Wheel
Bumper Cars
Big Dipper
Orbiter
Slingshot
Kingda Ka and Zumanjaro
Eejanaika
Fascinating Facts
Further Information
Glossary
Index

SKYSCRAPERS
Build It Tall
Home Insurance Building
Chrysler Building
Empire State Building
Willis Tower
Petronas Twin Tower
30 St Mary Axe
Taipei 101
Bahrain World Trade Center
Burj Khalifa
Bosco Verticale
Shanghai Tower
Fascinating Facts
Further Information
Glossary
Index

SPACECRAFTS
Out of This World!
Sputnik 1
Vostock 1
Apollo 11
Lunar Roving Vehicle
Voyager 1 and 2
Space Shuttle
Hubble Telescope
Rosetta Mission
International Space Station
Wilkinson Microwave Anisotropy Probe
Spirit and Opportunity Mars Rover
Fascinating Facts
Further Information
Glossary
Index

TRAINS, PLANES AND SHIPS
On the Move
Mary Rose
Washington Paddle Steamer
Stephenson's Rocket
SS Great Britain
Wright Flyer
Heinkel He 178
Shinkansen Bullet Train
Concorde
Shanghai Maglev Train
Airbus A380
USS Gerald R Ford (CVN 78)
Fascinating Facts
Further Information
Glossary
Index

TUNNELS
Going Underground
Thames Tunnel
New York City Subway
Holland Tunnel
Seikan Tunnel
Channel Tunnel
Oresund Tunnel
Laerdal Tunnel
Boston Big Dig Project
Smart Tunnel
Hadron Collider Tunnel
Gotthard Base Tunnel
Fascinating Facts
Further Information
Glossary
Index